Hang Gliding and Paragliding

Kelli Hicks

ROURKE PUBLISHING
Vero Beach, Florida

www.rourkepublishing.com

PHOTO CREDITS: © liteserv: title page; © MCarter: page 4; © Neale Cousland: page 5; © Wikipedia: page 6; © Library of Congress: pages 7, 8, 9; © Reinhold Foeger: page 11; © Drazen Vukelic: pages 11, 12, 13, 14; © creativephoto: page 15; © Dan Cardiff : page 15; © Sandro V. Maduell: page 16; © Alan Gordine: page 18; © Skyak: page 19; © John Todd: page 20a; © Nelson Hale: page 20b; © mariuspopma: © grybaz: page 21; © Gladysheva Sofiya: page 22

Edited by Jeanne Sturm

Cover and Interior designed by Tara Raymo

Library of Congress Cataloging-in-Publication Data

Hicks, Kelli.
  Hang gliding and paragliding / Kelli Hicks.
      p. cm. -- (Action sports)
  Includes index.
  ISBN 978-1-60694-357-1
  1. Hang gliding--Juvenile literature. 2. Paragliding--Juvenile literature.
I. Title.
  GV764.H53 2010
  797.5'5--dc22
                                    2009008952

www.rourkepublishing.com – rourke@rourkepublishing.com
Post Office Box 643328 Vero Beach, Florida 32964

TABLE OF CONTENTS

WHAT IS
Hang
Gliding?

Have you ever wondered how it feels to fly like a bird? If you are adventurous, you may try hang gliding. Hang gliding is an **aviation** sport where air currents help a pilot glide through the air. A pilot can easily fly 100 miles (160 kilometers) in a single flight.

DID YOU KNOW?

Hang gliding dates back to the sixth century. It is believed that China may be the site of the first hang gliding flights. The Emperor Wenxuan of the Northern Qi Dynasty launched his man-made kites from a tower. His pilots were prisoners who had been sentenced to death.

ACCOMPLISHMENTS IN
Aviation

Otto Lilienthal, a German aviation pioneer, was the first to make successful flights on a glider. He stated, "To invent an airplane is nothing. To build one is something. But to fly is everything." While working with his brother, he made more than 2,000 glider flights. A glider crash was ultimately the cause of his death. His work inspired the Wright brothers in their studies of aviation.

Otto Lilienthal

DID YOU KNOW?

Otto Lilienthal studied a variety of birds, especially storks, and modeled the wings of his glider on them. Because the glider attached to his shoulders, it was difficult to control the craft.

Orville Wright and his brother, Wilbur, opened a bicycle repair shop to fund their interest in flying. Their first designs were for gliders based on the Lilienthal designs. They later added an engine and received credit for creating the first airplanes.

With the many technological advances in flight and the addition of engine power, many people forgot about hang gliding. However, in the 1970s, designers decided to revisit the previous work and try to rejuvenate the sport.

The Wright brothers revised Otto Lilienthal's glider designs by adding a rudder to the tail and changing the shape of the wings. These modifications improved the length and quality of the flight.

| Sail |

| Frame |

| Control Bar |

Parts OF THE
Hang Glider

| Harness |

The frame of the hang glider is made of aluminum or **graphite** covered with fabric. The sail is a single piece of fabric that resembles the shape of wings. A typical wingspan is 30 feet (9 meters) with a weight of 45-80 pounds (20-36 kilograms). The pilot wears a **harness** that attaches under the glider. The pilot moves the **control bar** and shifts sideways to turn, or forward and backward to adjust the speed.

THE
Launch

In the early days of the sport, a pilot could only launch down hills and travel for limited distances. Today's gliders provide more options for pilots. A pilot can launch in one of three ways.

During a *foot launch*, a pilot faces into the wind and runs down a slope to become airborne.

A *towing launch* is suitable for flat regions. A vehicle or boat tows the glider until it reaches the desired altitude, then the pilot releases the tow rope.

During an *aerotow*, a small airplane called an **ultralight** tows the glider up 1,000-3,000 feet (305-915 meters) and releases it into the air.

A glider pilot needs to be aware of wind speed and lift changes during a foot launch.

WHAT IS Lift?

A glider flight can last for several hours. Pilots are able to maintain their altitude by using rising air to continue to glide. There are several different methods for maintaining **lift**.

Thermals are the most popular source of lift. The energy from the Sun heats the ground. The heat from the ground then heats the air. The warm air rises and lifts the wings into the air.

When the wind meets a mountain, cliff, or hill, the air pushes into the face of the mountain causing a *ridge lift*.

Convergence occurs when air masses meet and are forced upwards.

Hang Gliding

ARE HANG GLIDING
AND PARAGLIDING
The Same?

Many people think of hang gliding and paragliding as the same thing. They share many similarities, but they are completely different sports. The shape of a paraglider's wings change based on the flow of air through vents in the front of the wing. The pilot sits in a harness suspended from the wings.

Paragliding

WHAT IS Paragliding?

In 1963, Domina Jalbert applied to receive a patent for a **ram-air** design for a parachute with cells arranged in sections that would inflate while traveling through the air. At the same time, David Barish worked with NASA to develop a type of parachute called a **sail wing** that would help with the recovery of capsules dropped from rockets launched into space. By the 1970s, adventure seekers were using these parachutes combined with a foot launch, and the new sport of paragliding was introduced.

The International Hang Gliding and Paragliding Commission in Lausanne, Switzerland, governs all competitions in the sport. Australia hosted the first World Championship in 1975. In this annual event, which changes location each year, competitors test their skill in categories such as distance, accuracy, acrobatic maneuvers, and altitude.

Over time, technological advances brought changes to the shape and size of the sail. Modern paragliders no longer rely on the ram-air design, but instead depend on the flow of air past the outside surface of the wing. Wings generally have a wingspan of 26-40 feet (8-12 meters) and weigh approximately 6-15 pounds (3-7 kilograms). The speed of a paraglider is usually between 12-34 miles (20-60 kilometers) per hour.

DID YOU KNOW?

Some paragliders take the sport to the extreme. They attach a motor to their backs and use the engine power to increase the speed and intensity of the launch. The equipment and the motor can cost as much as $9,500.00!

HOW ARE HANG GLIDING AND PARAGLIDING Different?

Hang Gliding

Paragliding

	Hang Gliding	Paragliding
Wing structure	Rigid frame that does not collapse in windy conditions	Flexible wings that change shape based on the pressure of air; can collapse in windy conditions
Pilot position	Used lying in a prone position	Pilot sits in a supine position
Speed range	Faster: Up to 90+ miles per hour (145 kilometers per hour)	Slower: 12-34 miles per hour (20-60 kilometers per hour)
Landing	Longer approach and more landing area required	Smaller space needed
Instruction	Most instruction learned on the ground; some **tandem** instruction for in-air learning	Most skills learned in the air; tandem instruction rarely used
Convenience	More difficult to transport; attached to the roof of a vehicle	Lighter and easier to pack and carry; stored in the trunk of a car

NECESSARY
Technology

Both hang gliding and paragliding pilots use a variety of instruments to make their travels easier. It is difficult for pilots to know if the air is rising or falling. The **variometer** tracks vertical speed and helps them tell the difference. Pilots use airspeed indicators to determine their speed and two-way radios to communicate with ground crews. Some pilots, especially those who travel cross-country or participate in competitions, use a Global Positioning System (GPS) to track where they are going.

Two-way radio

Altimeter watch

Many people consider hang gliding and paragliding to be dangerous sports. Pilots carry a parachute in their harness in the event of an emergency, and most wear helmets while flying. Are you adventurous enough to try one of these exciting action sports?

GLOSSARY

aviation (ay-vee-AY-shuhn): the science of building and flying aircraft

control bar (kuhn-TROHL BAR): a long stick that makes the machine move in a particular direction

graphite (GRAF-ite): a common black or gray mineral

harness (HAR-nis): an arrangement of straps used to keep someone safe

lift (LIFT): to raise something or someone

ram-air (RAM-air): a type of parachute design that forms cells inflated by rising air

sail wing (SAYL WING): a single surface sail for a paraglider

tandem (TAN-duhm): two people, one behind the other, working in unison

ultralight (UHL-truh-lite): a very light aircraft, usually for one person, which is powered by a small engine

variometer (vair-ee-AH-muh-ter): an instrument used for measuring climb

INDEX

WEBSITES TO VISIT

http://howstuffworks.com/hang-gliding3.htm
http://howstuffworks.com/aviation-activities-for-kids.htm
www.academickids.com/encyclopedia/index.php/gliding
www.faa.gov/education_research/education/student_resources/kids_corner/
http://pbskids.org/dragonflytv/show/paragliding.html
http://members.tripod.com/~tekflight/allabout.html

ABOUT THE AUTHOR

Kelli Hicks is afraid of heights, but has great respect for those adventurers, like her cousin, who love the skies and enjoy the thrill of hang gliding. She lives with her husband and daughter in Tampa, Florida.